THE GRUFFALO PLAY

Written by Julia Donaldson

Illustrated by Axel Scheffler

First published 2014 by Macmillan Children's Books
a division of Macmillan Publishers Limited
20 New Wharf Road, London N1 9RR
Basingstoke and Oxford
Associated companies throughout the world
www.panmacmillan.com
www.gruffalo.com

ISBN: 978-1-4472-4309-0

Based on the bestselling picture book *The Gruffalo* by Julia Donaldson and Axel Scheffler

Play script first published in *The Gruffalo Theatre*
Face painting activity first published in *The Gruffalo Red Nose Day Book*

Text copyright © Julia Donaldson 1999, 2008, 2011, 2014
Illustrations copyright © Axel Scheffler 1999, 2008, 2011, 2014

Please contact Macmillan Children's Books for public performance rights.

1 3 5 7 9 8 6 4 2

A CIP catalogue record for this book is available from the British Library.
Printed in China

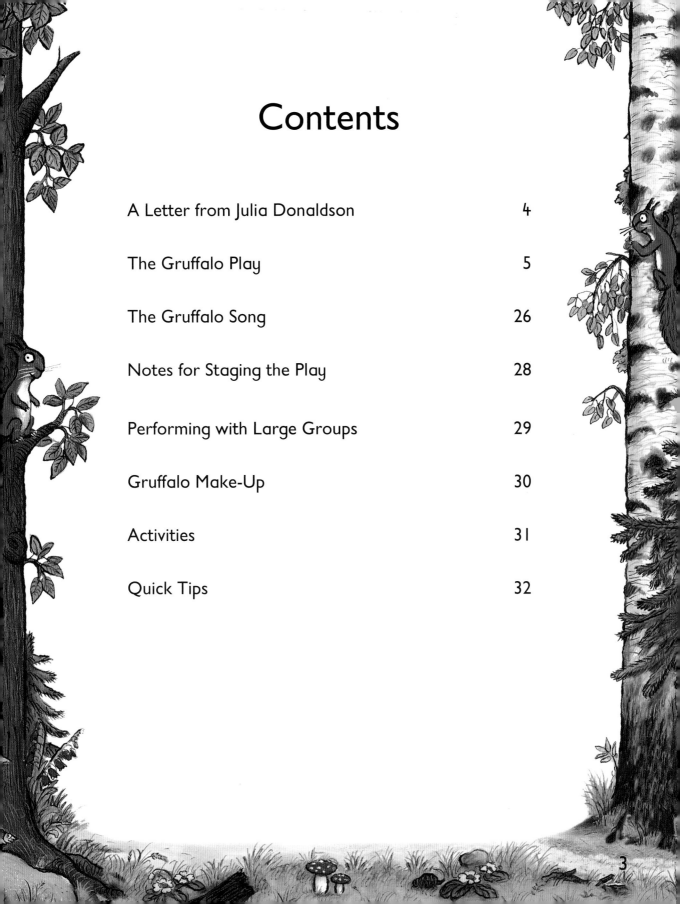

Contents

A Letter from Julia Donaldson

When I was little, my sister and I were always creating imaginary characters and putting on shows. And when I was a teenager I wanted to be an actress. Instead I became an author and wrote lots of books, but I've always loved the theatre, and writing and acting in plays too. During my two years as the Children's Laureate I created a website, www.picturebookplays.co.uk, to help children, parents and teachers enjoy acting out stories.

In this play book you'll find a script which you can use to put on your very own performance of *The Gruffalo*. There are fun ideas for putting on your play, as well as music and words from the Gruffalo song to add to your performance.

But now the lights are going down, the curtain is up and it's time for the show! I hope you have a wonderful time.

Julia Donaldson

The Characters

Narrator

Fox

Mouse

Snake

Owl

Gruffalo

Fox and Mouse enter from opposite sides of the stage

 A mouse took a stroll through the deep dark wood.
A fox saw the mouse and the mouse looked good.

 Where are you going to, little brown mouse?
Come and have lunch in my underground house.

 It's terribly kind of you, Fox, but no –
I'm going to have lunch with a gruffalo.

 A gruffalo? What's a gruffalo?

 A gruffalo! Why, didn't you know?
He has terrible tusks, and terrible claws,
And terrible teeth in his terrible jaws.

 Where are you meeting him?

 Here, by these rocks,
And his favourite food is roasted fox.

 Roasted fox! I'm off!

 Fox said.

 Goodbye, little mouse,

 and away he sped.

Exit Fox

 Silly old Fox! Doesn't he know,
There's no such thing as a gruffalo?

 On went the mouse through the deep dark wood.

Enter Owl

 An owl saw the mouse and the mouse looked good.

 Where are you going to, little brown mouse?
Come and have tea in my treetop house.

It's frightfully nice of you, Owl, but no —
I'm going to have tea with a gruffalo.

 A gruffalo? What's a gruffalo?

 A gruffalo! Why, didn't you know?
He has knobbly knees, and turned-out toes,
And a poisonous wart at the end of his nose.

 Where are you meeting him?

 Here, by this stream,
And his favourite food is owl ice cream.

 Owl ice cream? Toowhit toowhoo!
Goodbye, little mouse,

 and away Owl flew.

Exit Owl

 Silly old Owl! Doesn't he know,
There's no such thing as a gruffalo?

 On went the mouse through the deep dark wood.

Enter Snake

A snake saw the mouse and the mouse looked good.

Where are you going to, little brown mouse?
Come for a feast in my logpile house.

It's wonderfully good of you, Snake, but no –
I'm having a feast with a gruffalo.

A gruffalo? What's a gruffalo?

A gruffalo! Why, didn't you know?
His eyes are orange, his tongue is black;
He has purple prickles all over his back.

Where are you meeting him?

Here, by this lake,
And his favourite food is scrambled snake.

Scrambled snake! It's time I hid!
Goodbye, little mouse,

and away Snake slid.

Exit Snake
The Gruffalo enters slowly. Mouse doesn't see him

Silly old Snake! Doesn't he know,
There's no such thing as a gruffal . . .

Mouse suddenly sees Gruffalo
(in a shocked voice) **Oh!**

But who is this creature with terrible claws
And terrible teeth in his terrible jaws?
He has knobbly knees and turned-out toes
And a poisonous wart at the end of his nose.
His eyes are orange, his tongue is black;
He has purple prickles all over his back.

 Oh help! Oh no!
It's a gruffalo!

15

My favourite food!

 the Gruffalo said.

 You'll taste good on a slice of bread!

 Good?

 said the mouse.

 Don't call me good!
I'm the scariest creature in this wood.
Just walk behind me and soon you'll see,
Everyone is afraid of me.

16

(laughing) All right,

 said the Gruffalo, bursting with laughter.

 You go ahead and I'll follow after.

17

 They walked and walked till the Gruffalo said,

 I hear a hiss in the leaves ahead.

Enter Snake

 It's Snake,

said the mouse.

 Why, Snake, hello!

 Snake took one look at the Gruffalo.

 Oh crumbs!

 he said,

 Goodbye, little mouse,

 And off he slid to his logpile house.

Exit Snake

 You see?

 said the mouse.

 I told you so.

 Amazing!

said the Gruffalo.
They walked some more till the Gruffalo said,

 I hear a hoot in the trees ahead.

Enter Owl

 It's Owl,

 said the mouse.

 Why, Owl, hello!

 Owl took one look at the Gruffalo.

 Oh dear!

 he said,

 Goodbye, little mouse,

 And off he flew to his treetop house.

Exit Owl

 You see?

 said the mouse.

 I told you so.

 Astounding!

 said the Gruffalo.

 They walked some more till the Gruffalo said,

 I can hear feet on the path ahead.

Enter Fox

 It's Fox,

 said the mouse.

Why, Fox, hello!

 Fox took one look at the Gruffalo.

 Oh help!

 he said.

 Goodbye, little mouse,

 And off he ran to his underground house.

Exit Fox

Well, Gruffalo,

 said the mouse.

 You see?
Everyone is afraid of me!
But now my tummy's beginning to rumble.
My favourite food is – gruffalo crumble!

 Gruffalo crumble!

 the Gruffalo said,
And quick as the wind he turned and fled.

Exit Gruffalo

 All was quiet in the deep dark wood.
The mouse found a nut and the nut was good.

The Gruffalo Song

He has ter-ri-ble tusks and ter-ri-ble claws and ter-ri-ble teeth in his ter-ri-ble jaws. He's the Gruf-fa-lo, Gruf-fa-lo, Gruf-fa-lo. He's the Gruf-fa-lo.

He has knob-bl-y knees and turned-out toes and a poi-son-ous wart at the end of his nose. He's the Gruf-fa-lo, Gruf-fa-lo, Gruf-fa-lo. He's the Gruf-fa-lo.

His eyes are o-range. His tongue is black. He has pur-ple prick-les all o-ver his back. He's the Gruf-fa-lo, Gruf-fa-lo, Gruf-fa-lo. He's the Gruf-fa-lo, Gruf-fa-lo, Gruf-fa-lo. He's the Grr - rr - rr - rr - ruf-fa-lo,

HE'S THE GRUF-FA-LO!

26

He has terrible tusks

And terrible claws

And terrible teeth in his terrible jaws.

He's the Gruffalo, Gruffalo, Gruffalo,

He's the Gruffalo!

He has knobbly knees

And turned-out toes

And a poisonous wart at the end of his nose.

He's the Gruffalo, Gruffalo, Gruffalo,

He's the Gruffalo!

His eyes are orange.

His tongue is black.

He has purple prickles all over his back.

He's the Gruffalo, Gruffalo, Gruffalo.

He's the Gruffalo, Gruffalo, Gruffalo.

He's the Grr-rr-rr-rr-uffalo,

HE'S THE GRUFFALO!

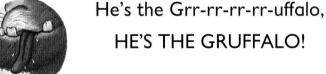

You could photocopy the song words, give a copy to everyone in your audience and have a singalong before or after your play. Or why not turn your play into a musical? When Mouse first sees the Gruffalo, instead of reading the narrator's lines you could sing the song!

Notes for Staging the Play

The Gruffalo can be performed by actors, or as a puppet show. Sets, props and costumes can be as simple or as complicated as you would like to make them. All the action takes place within the deep dark wood, so there's no need for any big scene changes.

Think about how the different characters move. How will you remind your audience that Owl can fly? Will Snake really slide about, or wiggle as he walks in, or might the actor use a puppet?

Plan the sides from which your characters will enter and exit the stage. Should Snake, Owl and Fox enter from the same sides, or from different directions?

Why not add atmospheric sound effects, like owl hoots and gruffalo footsteps?

Performing with Large Groups

There are six speaking roles in *The Gruffalo*, but it can easily be performed by larger groups too. Here are two simple ways you can involve everyone.

Divide up the narrator's part between two or more actors, then lots of people can join in.

Alternatively, choose one person to be the mouse and one to be the Gruffalo. Everyone else can be divided into groups of foxes, owls and snakes. They can either speak in unison, or the lines can be shared.

You may find it helpful to give each group a "den" or corner of the stage. They should stay in these areas throughout the play, emerging to prowl around – or run away from – the mouse. This is easier and speedier than moving groups on and off stage.

Gruffalo Make-Up

If you decide to go all the way and dress up in costumes to perform your play, you could use face paints too. Here are some ideas for the mouse and the Gruffalo. Can you design your own for the other characters?

Gruffalo

- Paint the actor's face brown.
- Add white tusks and a big black tongue.
- Don't forget the white teeth and green wart.
- You could make ears and horns from card.
- What a scary Gruffalo!

The mouse

- Paint a little pink nose.
- Add some whiskers and a small mouth.
- Make some ears from card or paper plates.
- You could even use a long sock for a tail.

Activities

Posters

Remember to let people know that your play is happening! Write where your performance will be and when it will start.

Tickets

Why not design tickets for your audience? Make enough for everyone who wants to come and watch. Remember to check the tickets when your audience arrives.

Programmes

Your programme tells the audience who the actors are and it's a great souvenir. Fold a piece of paper in half to make your programme, then write the name of the play on the front and decorate it. That's the cover! Inside, write a list of the characters and who is playing them. Then add the names of everyone else who is helping with the play but who isn't acting. You could add drawings too.

Quick Tips

 Remember that practice makes perfect. Rehearse before your big performance.

 Practise your lines and ask someone to test you as you learn them.

 Knowing who speaks just before you and listening to what they say is called a cue. It's very important to know when you should speak, so remember to learn your cues too.

 Don't forget to take a big bow at the end!

 Caught the acting bug? Visit www.picturebookplays.co.uk for more play ideas.